SCOTT JOPLIN
& the Age of Ragtime

The Life, Times & Music® Series

The Life, Times & Music® Series

Timothy Frew

FRIEDMAN/FAIRFAX
PUBLISHERS

Dedication

To Dorothy Susanne Grimes (Mama Dot),
the finest ragtime piano player in Stanford, Kentucky.

A FRIEDMAN/FAIRFAX BOOK

© 1996 Friedman/Fairfax Publishers

ISBN 1-56799-304-4

Editor: Tony Burgess
Art Director: Jeff Batzli
Designer: Susan E. Livingston
Layout: Ruth Diamond
Photography Editor: Colleen Branigan
Production Manager: Jeanne E. Kaufman

Grateful acknowledgment is given to authors, publishers, and photographers for
permission to reprint material. Every effort has been made to determine copyright
owners of photographs and illustrations. In the case of any omissions, the publishers will be pleased to make suitable acknowledgments in future editions.

Color separation by HK Scanner Arts Int'l Ltd.
Printed in Hong Kong and bound in China by Midas Printing Limited

For bulk purchases and special sales, please contact:
Friedman/Fairfax Publishers
Attention: Sales Department
15 West 26th Street
New York, New York 10010
(212) 685-6610   FAX (212) 685-1307
Website: http://www.webcom.com/friedman/

Contents

Introduction:
What Is Ragtime?

Ragtime is one of America's earliest and most unique contributions to the musical canon. In its classic form, it is instrumental piano music characterized by highly intricate syncopated melodies set against a straight march-type, or oompah, bass line. It usually consists of three or four distinct sections, or themes, each a self-contained entity made up of sixteen measures. After breaking on the scene in the 1890s, piano ragtime was adapted into ragtime songs, music for small combos and brass bands, ragtime waltzes, and novelty rags. At the heart of all these variations is the ever-present syncopation that gave ragtime, or "ragged time," its name.

When most people think of ragtime, they think of "The Entertainer," that catchy Scott Joplin (1868–1917) tune made famous by the 1973 movie The Sting and heard all summer long in clunky electronic versions emanating from countless ice cream vans and mechanical hobbyhorses. They may also think of sharply dressed men sitting around a smoky poker table and drinking whiskey while a piano player pounds out a few "rags" on an old upright.

Ragtime is and always was a musical form associated with high energy and good times. It was born in saloons and bordellos, and it was a big part of what made the "Gay Nineties" sound so gay. The ragtime craze hit full stride during the first fifteen years of the twentieth century, becoming—along with its Tin Pan Alley variants, vocal and novelty ragtime—the most popular form of music in the world.

What made this so amazing was the fact that ragtime was essentially an African-American form of music, pioneered by innovators such as Scott Joplin, Tom Turpin (1873–1922), Louis Chauvin (1883–1908), and hundreds of other African-American itinerant piano players who traveled from saloon to saloon playing for tips.

Because ragtime developed before music was recorded and few of its earliest innovators had their songs published, it is difficult to pinpoint exactly when the form started. The first published sheet music with "rag" in the title appeared in the mid-1890s, but the syncopation that gives ragtime its character can be traced back to African rhythmic dances brought to America on slave ships. If not for the institution of slavery and its underlying racism, we might never have had ragtime

By the end of the nineteenth century, a short stretch of 28th Street in Manhattan was the center of the U.S. music industry. It became known as Tin Pan Alley because of the "tinny" sounds of piano music coming from the hundreds of small offices.

music. While its roots are primarily African-American, the intermingling of African syncopation with Euro-American folk music was crucial to ragtime's development. Ragtime is the result of a long and complex tradition of white and black musicians repeatedly imitating, borrowing, and parodying each other's musical forms. In order to truly understand ragtime and how it came about, we need to carefully examine the history of syncopated music and the unique phenomena of race and music in America, all leading up to the creation of one of the most popular musical genres of all time—ragtime music.

The Roots of Syncopation

African syncopated rhythmic dances such as the Bamboula, Calinda, Chacta, Babouille, and Counjaille were transported to America via slave ships. This African musical tradition blended with Euro-American folk songs on plantations throughout the South, resulting in the musical hybrids of the work song, the spiritual, and the shout song. It is here that the first strains of syncopated music entered the American folk idiom, starting the musical lineage that would later develop into ragtime, blues, and, eventually, jazz and rock and roll.

During the era that preceded the Civil War, whites developed a fascination with African-American music and dance, and with black culture in general. White composers and entertainers appropriated elements of African-American folk music for use in their own compositions. Every Sunday, blacks were allowed to gather in La Place Congo, or Congo Square, in New Orleans to perform chants, shouts, and dances from their native Africa. It was in Congo Square that the purest forms of

The Bamboula was one of the the many African dances performed on Congo Square in New Orleans. The dance inspired a syncopated piano piece of the same name by composer Louis Moreau Gottschalk.

African music and dance were preserved for many decades.

In 1847, eighteen-year-old Louis Moreau Gottschalk (1829–1869), the son of an English cotton broker and a French Creole mother, wrote "La Bamboula— Danse de Negres," an extremely complicated piano piece influenced by the Bamboula dance

Louis Moreau Gottschalk (1829-1869) was the first American composer to use African rhythms and syncopation in his works.

he saw in Congo Square. A prodigy at the age of fifteen, Gottschalk had earlier established his musical credibility with a concert at the Salle Pleyel in Paris, where he was enthusiastically received by Frédéric Chopin (1810–1849). Although it was written fifty years before the first published ragtime piece, "La Bamboula" contains many of the same syncopations and polyrhythms that later gave ragtime music its unique and distinctive character.

Like Gottschalk, Stephen Collins Foster (1826–1864) was a white composer who used African-American melodies and rhythms in his work. Unlike Gottschalk, whose compositions were firmly grounded in the European classical tradition, Foster was very much a popular songwriter who consciously wrote imitations of the river and field songs of black America. Dubbed "America's first songwriter," Foster was so successful that he was able to demand a percentage of the sales from his sheet music, making him the first songwriter ever to receive royalties.

Many of his "Negro" songs were extensively used in minstrel shows for the next thirty years, but he never felt completely comfortable with his black imitation and minstrel songs. When Edwin Christy (1815–1862) began using "Old Folks at Home" in his minstrel show, Foster asked that he not be credited for the song. After Christy made the song famous and it began to sell, Foster demanded that his name be printed on the cover of the sheet music, which prompted Christy to call Foster a "vacillating skunk." Years after Foster's death, many of his compositions, such as "Jeanie with the Light Brown Hair," "O Susanna," and "Old Folks at Home," were mistaken for authentic black folk songs.

The white fascination with African-American music and culture culminated with the development of the minstrel show

A piece of the score of Louis Gottschalk's "The Bamboula," complete with Creole lyrics.

in the 1830s. Thomas "Daddy" Rice (1808–1860), dubbed "The Father of American Minstrelsy," introduced his infamous Jim Crow character in 1832 at the Bowery Theater in New York City. Legend has it that four years earlier this marginal actor was at a stable in Louisville when he witnessed the song and dance performance of an old and arthritic black horse groom. Rice immediately saw the comic possibilities of such a character, and adopted the groom's song, dance, and tattered clothes. With the addition of a little burnt cork to blacken his white face, Rice created "Jump Jim Crow."

In all likelihood, however, Rice actually stole his character from a popular black street musician. The real Jim Crow was not a shuffling, cowardly comic at all, but an extremely successful entertainer. The survivor of a slave uprising, Jim Crow eventually made enough money to settle down in Virginia with his white wife.

Rice's character became so popular that other white entertainers soon began imitating him. Eventually, entire troupes of so-called "Ethiopian Delineators" sprang up, giving birth to America's first native theatrical form—the minstrel show.

Stephen Foster (1826-1864) was considered America's first popular songwriter. Many of his songs were imitations of the river and field songs of black America.

The minstrel show, performed by white "Ethiopian Delineators" in black face, was the first theatrical form developed in the United States.

Eventually, Jim Crow became such a ubiquitous American icon that by the late 1890s the term *Jim Crow* was a common pejorative term evoking the stereotype of the lazy, stupid, and cowardly southern black, and the segregationist statutes that were passed in southern states at this time were referred to as Jim Crow laws.

The
Minstrel Show

During and before the 1830s, black entertainers on southern plantations would stage elaborate variety shows consisting of jokes, dancing, and songs accompanied by the banjo and the "bones" (dried horse ribs used for percussion). Once the Ethiopian Delineators gained popularity, white entertainers incorporated the plantation variety shows into the minstrel show. The original minstrel form, as developed by such barnstorming troupes as the Edwin Christy Minstrels, was a blend of predictable clean comedy and watered-down African-American folk music and dance. The shows themselves adhered to a rigid format that left little room for variation. The day usually began with a noon parade and concert, known simply as "the march" (marches were extremely popular during the mid-1800s, when John Philip Sousa [1854–1932] was the most famous musician in the world). As with the carnival or circus parade, the minstrel march was a device used to attract audiences for the real show later that night.

At the minstrel show's center was Mr. Interlocutor, who served as the master of ceremonies. The show began with a comic repartee between Mr. Interlocutor and his two end men, Bruder Tambo and Bruder Bones (the banjo player and the percussionist). This was followed by the olio, or variety, segment of the show, which consisted of jokes, songs, and dances, and the show ended with a one-act skit. (In the

During the 1800s, the music and culture of black America became popular among whites. This sketch by John N. Hyde depicts "wandering African Minstrels performing at a noted place of resort on Harlem Lane."

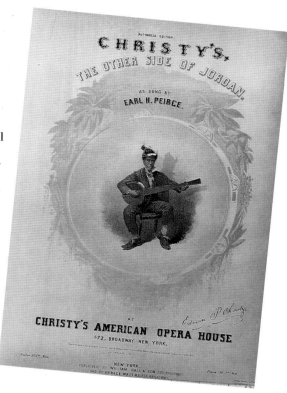

1890s, when the minstrel show declined into nothing more than a commercial showcase for vicious racist humor, the format for the olio portion of the show was lifted and developed into vaudeville.) The show's finale was the Grand Walk segment. This was the high-stepping dance parade at the

Performers' likenesses were often printed on the front of sheet music to increase sales. Here Earl Peirce of the Edwin Christy Minstrels is shown in full blackface regalia.

end of the show, which later evolved into the cakewalk craze that swept the country in the 1890s.

While the minstrel show borrowed from, parodied, and sometimes celebrated black music and culture, no black minstrel troupes existed until after Emancipation. In the few cases where black performers were part of a white minstrel troupe, they never shared a stage with whites and were usually forced to cover their faces with burnt cork, becoming caricatures of themselves.

In the 1870s, just as minstrelsy hit its prime, a white man named W.H. Lee started the first all-black minstrel show, boasting "fifteen ex-slaves performing pure plantation melodies." All-black minstrel shows were known as "Georgia Minstrels" to distinguish them from their more popular white-in-blackface counterparts. Soon other white-owned (and even a few black-owned) Georgia Minstrel shows began touring the country, and for the first time blacks performed professionally for white audiences.

The Lew Dockstrader Minstrels featured a young singer named Al Jolson. Jolson would continue to perform in black face into the 1930s.

This new freedom to perform came with a price. The minstrel show had burned the image of the lazy, dishonest, immoral, gluttonous, and stupid black man deep into the public consciousness. The black musicians and actors who wanted to perform for white audiences had to adhere to the acceptable racial stereotypes for success. After 1875, minstrel shows got nastier and, in turn, more popular. This development coincided with a steep increase in racial hatred, brought on in part by the failures of Reconstruction, and in part by the crude yet popular interpretation of Charles Darwin's theory of evolution, which placed the white Anglo-Saxon at the top of the evolutionary ladder and those with darker skin and of African descent at the bottom. By the 1890s, just as the black artistic and musical community had begun to make innovative strides, violent racial hatred in the United States hit its peak: between 1889 and 1899, there were 1,460 reported lynchings in the United States.

The Cakewalk and the Coon Song

Black minstrel performers and traveling musicians gradually began to stretch the rigid boundaries of the medium by adding their own unique interpretations to the songs they were performing. They found artistic expression by "ragging" the songs—playing them in "ragged time."

In Terry Waldo's excellent book *This Is Ragtime*, the author quotes Eubie Blake (1883–1983) reminiscing about his childhood in Baltimore, Maryland: "I used to hear the colored band going to funerals. On the way over they'd play the funeral march straight, but coming back they'd rag the hell out of the music. So I started playing music like that."

Black performers also changed the minstrel format by emphasizing the cake-walk segment of the show, adding more and more synco-pation to the music and per-forming increasingly elaborate and energetic high-stepping dances. The cakewalk dates back to pre–Civil War days, when slaves would perform comic and exaggerated imi-tations of their masters' ballroom

Eubie Blake (1883–1983) had the longest career of any of the great ragtime players. He grew up listening to marching bands "rag" the standard marches of John Philip Sousa, among others.

17

The high-stepping cakewalk was a huge dance and music craze in the 1890s.

dances. The slaves would dress in top-hat finery (or an imitation thereof) and parade around performing a high-stepping dance. Enamored of this mocking dance, plantation owners began holding competitions among their slaves, awarding a cake to the best performers.

The early white minstrel innovators used their interpretation of the cakewalk as the finale to their shows. When blacks started performing in minstrel shows, they further refined the dance. By the 1890s, the cakewalk had become a national craze, with competitions held across the country; yearly national championships were held at Madison Square Garden in New York.

The cakewalk's popularity was the result of an odd cultural exchange. In a country steeped in racial segregation, during a period when racial hatred was at its worst, the cakewalk and its accompanying music evolved from a complex chain of racial parody. It was a dance competition for whites who were imitating the black minstrels, who, in turn, had adopted it from the white minstrels, who were imitating the way black slaves parodied their white masters.

Since the cakewalk was primarily an instrumental form of music and dance, it was inherently less offensive than another popular form of music that evolved directly from the minstrel show—the "coon song."

The coon song first entered the country's musical consciousness in the mid-1880s, and exploded onto the public scene in 1896 with the release of the immensely popular and equally hated "All Coons Look Alike to Me" by Ernest Hogan. While coon songs did contain some rudimentary syncopation, they were a far cry from ragtime. Songs such as "Syncopated Sambo," "Mammy's Little Pumpkin-Colored Coons," "Gentle Coon Deviation," "I Wants to Live While I'm Living Cos I'se Agoin' to Be a Long Time Dead," and "All Coons Look Alike to Me" were little more than new ways to derive humor from the stereotype of the lazy black man.

"All Coons Look Alike to Me" quickly became one of the biggest hits of the 1890s, with its sheet music selling more than one million copies. As popular as it was with the white public, it was even more ve-

hemently despised by blacks. Ironically, Ernest Hogan, the song's writer, was a black man. Taken literally, the song is not quite as offensive as the title may indicate. It tells the story of a black woman who leaves her lover because she has fallen in love with an-other. The chorus of the song means that all blacks look alike to her except for her new love.

Hogan got the inspiration for the song when visit-ing the sporting district in

Ernest Hogan was an accomplished black performer and songwriter who became infamous when he penned the smash hit "All Coons Look Alike to Me."

Ben Harney (1871–1938)

On February 16, 1896, a twenty-five-year-old entertainer named Benjamin R. Harney took the stage at Keith's Union Square Theater in New York City. Wearing a ragged straw hat and battered bamboo cane draped over his left arm, Harney rushed to the stage and enthusiastically addressed the audience: "Folks, I'm Ben Harney from Louisville, and I'm announcing a new epoch in Ethiopian minstrelsy. Old Black Joe may roll in his grave, but I'm giving you the real thing in ragtime, and I mean ragtime!"

With that announcement, Harney, along with his two sidekicks—his wife Jessie and a young black man named Strap Hill—launched into a musical review of no-holds-barred, exuberant, syncopated music the likes of which no New York vaudeville audience had ever seen.

Thus began a long successful run at Keith's Theater followed by an equally successful run at the larger Tony Pastor's Theater, in which Harney billed himself as the "Inventor of Ragtime."

Born to a white Kentucky family, Ben Harney could have easily followed his father into the life of a successful, middle-class professional. His parents sent him to private school and then to a military academy, but Harney fell in love with the piano, especially the syncopated music he heard coming from the Louisville sporting district.

By the age of seventeen Harney was already a regular at the bars and sporting houses of Louisville. Harney soon took his act on the road, barnstorming across the midwest, including a stop at the Columbian Exposition in Chicago in 1893.

By this point, Harney had written two of the most popular songs in his act, "You've Been A Good Old Wagon, But You've Done Broke Down" and "Mr. Johnson, Turn Me Loose," but he was unsure of how to score their syncopated melodies, and was unable to get the songs published. Back in Louisville, Harney met Johnny Biller, the musical director at Macauley's Theater. Biller transcribed the two songs directly from a Harney performance. Unfortunately, a disgruntled employee named Harry Green stole the score for "Mr. Johnson, Turn Me Loose" and sold it to W.G. Warren, an Indiana publisher. While Green took credit for writing the song, he did dedicate it to Harney with an inscription that read, "Sung with much success by Ben R. Harney." The Green version of "Mr. Johnson" was simplified to eliminate all syncopation.

In 1895, "You've Been a Good Old Wagon..." was published by Bruner Greenup in Louisville. Although the song is a far cry from the classic ragtime of Scott Joplin, is it generally recognized as one of the first syncopated songs ever to be published. The first instrumental rags, William Krell's "Mississippi Rag" and Tom Turpin's "Harlem Rag," were not published until more than a year later.

Just prior to his appearance at Keith's Theater, Harney sold his own version of "Mr. Johnson, Turn Me Loose"—complete with syncopation—to the Tin Pan Alley publisher F.K. Harding.

Harney's runaway success at Keith's and Tony Pastor's caught the eye of the powerhouse Tin Pan Alley publisher M. Witmark & Sons. Witmark sensed that ragtime was poised to take the country by storm, and they knew that Harney had been working on an instructional book on ragtime. The company bought the rights to Harney's first two songs and his book.

In 1897, Witmark published Ben Harney's *Ragtime Instructor*. On the cover of the book Harney describes himself, with characteristic immodesty, as "Original Instructor to the Stage of the Now Popular Rag Time in Ethiopian Song."

B en Harney was a tireless performer and the self-proclaimed "Inventor of Ragtime." His greatest asset may have been his talent for self-promotion.

Throughout Harney's long career, he billed himself either as the "Originator" or the "Inventor" of ragtime. While he was a talented piano player in the ragtime vein and he did much to popularize the term ragtime, his songs were not true ragtime in the Joplin sense. They were more or less highly syncopated "coon songs" or cakewalks, with elements of both ragtime and the blues.

More than anything, Harney was a top-notch vaudeville entertainer. He tirelessly toured the world several times over preaching the wonders of ragtime, until a heart attack in 1923 made performing difficult. In 1930, Harney and his wife Jessie retired to a small flat in Philadelphia. Harney died penniless eight years later, still believing that he was the true "Inventor of Ragtime."

Chicago. There he heard a black saloon entertainer perform a song entitled "All Pimps Look Alike to Me." Hogan altered the chorus and wrote a new verse; with an arrangement by Max Hoffman, the song went on to launch the coon-song craze. Hogan, however, spent the rest of his life apologizing for the song. Once he even tried to defend it by saying it was not about blacks at all, but raccoons. In 1896, Irving Jones, one of the most prolific black writers of coon songs, penned a parody of Hogan's hit called "All Birds Look Like Chickens to Me."

While the cakewalk and the coon song were introducing syncopation to the general public, a vastly different, yet related form of music could be heard coming from the saloons, bordellos, and "sporting houses" across the Midwest. It is at these places that traveling pianists would gather to exchange ideas and licks, and hold informal competitions to see who could "out-rag" whom on the piano.

The coon song, along with the cakewalk, introduced syncopation into popular song, paving the way for the runaway success of ragtime music.

The World's Columbian Exposition, which opened in 1893, was the destination of countless itinerant ragtime piano players.

The World's
Columbian Exposition

The Funky Butt Hall, Odd Fellows Hall, the Rosebud, the Maple Leaf, the Hurrah, Nellie Halls, the "400" Club—these and hundreds of other sporting clubs, bordellos, and saloons were the collective birthplace of ragtime music. Throughout the later part of the nineteenth century, hundreds of itinerant musicians traveled from one sporting district to another across the Midwest and the Mississippi River basin, going where life was fast, money was good, and music went on until the wee hours of the morning.

Ragtime evolved from live performance. It was a way of breaking from established musical conventions by adding showy syncopation and

While many of the exhibits at the Expo were quite grand, the real action took place in the saloons along the Midway, where musical history was being made.

complicated rhythms to bland contemporary music. The sporting districts were places where pianists would gather, exchange ideas, and challenge each other to informal "cutting" competitions to see who could come up with the best rag version of a popular song.

Before long these musicians were creating their own ragtime compositions, which were often so complex and unconventional that early efforts to put them to sheet music proved difficult. Also, no ragtime player played a piece of music the same way twice. Even Scott Joplin, who would later print instructions on his sheet music declaring that the notes should be played as written, added several "unwritten" bass flourishes to his early piano roll performances.

While ragtime (if not the word to describe it) was around for much of the late 1800s, it did not make it to sheet music until nearly the turn of the century, and was not even heard outside of the sporting districts until 1893—the year that the city of Chicago hosted the World's Columbian Exposition.

In 1892, the buzz around the sporting circuit was about the upcoming exposition in Chicago, the largest and most elaborate world's fair since London initiated the trend with the Crystal Palace Exhibition in 1851. The World's Columbian Exposition was a celebration of culture and technology (an early version of the motion picture camera was demonstrated there). Most important to the itinerant musicians, the Expo included a mile-long (1.6km) entertainment strip called the Midway. Because of the Midway and the hundreds of temporary saloons and bordellos that sprang up on the outskirts of the fair, Chicago was clearly the place to be for any traveling musician.

With the opening of the fair in 1893, hundreds of banjo players, marching bands, minstrel performers, coon shouters, and pianists descended upon the Windy City. Among them was Plunk Henry, an early ragtime pioneer from Mississippi whose nickname came from his banjo style, but by the time of the Exposition, Plunk had switched to the piano. He had developed the rudiments of piano ragtime from his natural banjo syncopation. For Plunk, ragtime came simply from trying to play his banjo licks on the piano.

W.C. Handy (1873–1958), who would one day be hailed as "The Father of the Blues," performed at the Expo with Maholy's Minstrels. Handy later formed his first quartet in Chicago, and performed both at the fair and in the sporting district.

The Columbian Exposition also drew the interest of a serious young African-American musician from Texarkana, Texas, by the name of Scott Joplin. It was on the Midway that the twenty-five-year-old Joplin met Otis Saunders, a fellow pianist who became Joplin's closest friend and, for several years, his unofficial advisor and manager. Scott Joplin was in Chicago for the same reason that hundreds of others were there: to work the saloons on the fringes of the fairgrounds, meet other musicians, and make a few bucks.

The Exposition also played host to several exhibitions and shows that celebrated both African and African-American music. These were not the white-men-in-blackface send-ups featured in minstrel shows; they represented the closest thing to true black music that white America had ever heard.

On the Midway, the Creole Show played to packed houses every night. This was one of the first all-black troupes to play almost exclusively for white audiences. What made this even more remarkable was that the Creole Show was done without blackface. The popularity of the show was no doubt increased by the presence of scantily clad, light-skinned Creole dancers.

Other popular attractions were the Cairo Street concession, which put on African, Sudanese, and Egyptian shows, and the Dahomean Village, a reproduction of an African village where native West Africans entertained the white audiences with drumming, chants, and dances from their African homeland. While the exhibit was wildly popular with white America, many educated African-Americans who saw or heard about the Dahomean Village were actually quite offended. At a time when they were struggling for intellectual and artistic respect, the Dahomean Village portrayed blacks as primitive and uncivilized.

The Columbian Exposition was a landmark event in the development of ragtime. It gave the public its first taste of this burgeoning musical form, but perhaps more importantly, it was also a meeting place for contemporary black musicians to exchange ideas and styles. In essence, this was the same thing that was going on in the sporting districts across the Midwest, but in Chicago, the musical exchange was on a much larger scale. Instead of a few musicians sitting around a lone piano trading licks, there were literally hundreds of musicians in Chicago, each with his own unique style and musical vision.

Many of ragtime's earliest innovators were more interested in moneymaking live performance than they were in composing their own music, and this tended to slow the development of ragtime as a legitimate musical form. While many of the itinerants had great musical talent, their ambitions—and many times their opportunities—rarely went beyond the next saloon.

Scott Joplin changed all that. With a studious demeanor and grim determination, Joplin attempted to shed ragtime's reputation as good-time saloon music and to move it into the realm of serious art. A few years after the Exposition, he penned his first ragtime composition. By the turn of the century, Joplin would be known as "The King of the Ragtime Writers."

Composer of "St. Louis Blues" and "Memphis Blues," later to be dubbed "the father of the blues," W.C. Handy performed at the Columbian Exposition as part of Mahoney's Minstrels.

A soft-spoken man from Texarkana, Texas, Scott Joplin (1868-1917) was the single most influential composer of classic ragtime.

Scott Joplin
and Sedalia, Missouri

After leaving Chicago, Scott Joplin and his new friend Otis Saunders traveled to Sedalia, Missouri—a former frontier town of fifteen thousand people that, because of its large sporting district and enormous black population, was one of the early hotbeds of ragtime music.

Sedalia was established in 1860 as a Union military outpost. After the war, it was a booming frontier town; by 1896 it was the Pettis County seat as well as the terminus of four divisions of the Missouri Pacific Railroad. Along with the railroad came prosperity and jobs, and soon Sedalia was the destination of thousands of African-Americans looking for a better life.

Otis Saunders was good friends with Will and Walker Williams, two brothers who ran the Maple Leaf Club, the premier sporting house in Sedalia's tenderloin district. The Maple Leaf Club contained an old oak Victorian bar, several pool and gambling tables, and a well-worn upright piano. Its patrons included both blacks and whites, all of whom were there to gamble, drink, and have a good time. The Maple Leaf also had a reputation as a place for music and was a regular stop of itinerant piano players. Both Joplin and Saunders became regular players at the Maple Leaf, playing all night long for $1.50 plus tips.

With the encouragement of the Williams brothers, Joplin entered the George Smith College of Music, where he studied composition. At the time, he was living with the family of a fellow student, Arthur Marshall. Joplin and Marshall would eventually collaborate on two ragtime classics: "Swipesy Cakewalk" and "The Lily Queen."

It was in Sedalia that Joplin perfected his distinctive ragtime style and began writing his first compositions. Considering his passion for ragtime, it is surprising that Joplin's first two published songs, "Please Say You Will" and "Picture of Her Face," were sentimental ballads with no syncopation at all.

Unlike many other ragtime pioneers who weren't interested in composition, Joplin became obsessed with scoring the complex syncopations of this new musical form. He saw ragtime as a complex art form, worthy of the same respect as classical music. He lived for the day when his music would transcend the saloons and alight in the civilized drawing rooms and gilded concert halls of upper-crust America.

By 1897, the first three instrumental rags made it into published sheet music: William Krell's "Mississippi Rag," Tom Turpin's "Harlem Rag," and Paul Sarebresole's "Roustabout Rag." ("Louisiana Rag," by Theodore H. Northrup, was also published that year, but despite its name, this song is not considered true ragtime.) While these early published ragtime pieces were not commercially successful, they were instrumental in putting the word "ragtime" in the public consciousness. Musically, they took a breezy, untutored approach that was true to their performance roots. These original rag pieces were much more spontaneous and less polished than the music Joplin was working on.

By 1898 Joplin had completed his first two ragtime compositions, "Original Rags" and "Maple Leaf Rag," the latter named in honor of the Williams brothers' club. The two songs became popular on the Sedalia music circuit, encouraging Joplin to look for a publisher. His first stop was A.W. Perry & Son, Sedalia's largest music store and publishing house, where he was summarily rejected. Joplin then went to Kansas City, where he played the two songs for Charles N. Daniels of the Carl Hoffman Publishing Company. Daniels was so taken by Joplin's work that he encouraged Hoffman to buy both pieces. The wary Hoffman, however, decided to take a chance only on "Original Rags." He passed on "Maple Leaf Rag."

"Original Rags" was published in March 1899. The cover depicts an old black plantation worker picking up rags in front of a cabin. Under the title is printed "Picked by Scott Joplin. Arranged by Chas. N. Daniels." Charles N. Daniels later moved to Detroit and then to New York City, where he managed Jerome H. Remick & Co., one of Tin Pan Alley's largest publishers. In the decade prior to 1912, Remick & Co. published more than five hundred rags, making them by far the largest publisher of ragtime music.

The original sheet music cover for Joplin's first published rag, "Original Rags." Charles Daniels, the first publisher to believe in Joplin, went on to great success on Tin Pan Alley.

Having published his first rag, Joplin enjoyed newfound fame in Sedalia. Soon piano players of every ilk were searching him out for lessons and advice. One of Joplin's early protégés was Scott Hayden. A Sedalia native, Hayden was attending Lincoln High School when Joplin met him. With Joplin as tutor, Hayden honed his ragtime and composition skills. Like Arthur Marshall before him, Scott Hayden collaborated with Joplin on several rags: "Sunflower Slow Drag" (1901), "Something Doing" (1903), "Felicity Rag" (1911), and "Kismet Rag" (1913).

Hayden also introduced Joplin to his widowed sister-in-law, Belle Hayden. One year later the two were married. According to John Stark,

Nicknamed "The Ragtime Kid," S. Brunson Campbell was a teenage runaway who learned to play ragtime from Scott Joplin and Otis Saunders.

"Sunflower Slow Drag" was a testament to Joplin's love for Belle: "This piece came to light during the high temperature of Scott Joplin's courtship, and while he was touching the ground only in the highest places. His geese were all swans and Mississippi water tasted like honeydew....Hold your ear to the ground while someone plays it, and you can hear Scott Joplin's heart beat."

S. Brunson Campbell, a white teenager from Washington, Kansas, was another young ragtime hotshot who sought out Joplin. At the age of fourteen, Campbell ran away from home to Oklahoma City, where he wandered into a music store and began to play the piano. A crowd soon gathered as he ran through the popular tunes of the day. Joplin's good friend and fellow musician Otis Saunders happened to be in the store and hear Campbell play. According to Campbell, "He came over to the piano and placed a pen-and-ink manuscript of a piece of music in front of me and asked if I would play it." It was "Maple Leaf Rag."

A few months later, Campbell went to Sedalia to seek out Joplin and Saunders. After hearing Campbell play, Joplin agreed to be his teacher. "He taught me to play his first two rags, 'Original Rags' and 'Maple Leaf.' Joplin and Saunders nicknamed me 'The Ragtime Kid,' and that name was to stick with me all through my ragtime career."

One afternoon while Joplin was playing at the Maple Leaf Club, the Williams brothers introduced him to a white music store owner named John Stark. Stark was as taken by Joplin's fierce dedication as he was by his smooth playing. The next day Joplin went down to Stark's music store and played "Maple Leaf Rag" for him. Stark bought the song on the spot, thus beginning a friendship and publishing partnership that would last for the remaining eighteen years of Joplin's life.

John Stark, with young wife Sarah Ann and infant son Etilman in tow, had moved to Missouri in 1868 to set up a frontier farm. Stark quickly grew tired of the difficult farming life and moved his family to the town of Chilicothe, where he opened an ice cream business. He was an excellent traveling salesman and his business prospered. While on his sales route, Stark consigned a cabinet organ from Jesse French, a St. Louis music store owner. Stark carried the organ with him during his rounds and eventually sold it. With the money he bought another organ and a piano and sold them. Stark became so successful at selling organs and pianos that he forsook his ice cream business and set up a music shop in the growing railroad town of Sedalia.

"Maple Leaf Rag" was Stark's first venture into sheet music publishing. He paid Joplin fifty dollars plus royalties for the song—a very good deal considering it was unheard of at the time to offer royalties to black songwriters. The sheet music went on sale in September 1899, and with Joplin promoting it, the rag became extremely popular across Missouri. Through word of mouth, the song's popularity spread, and over the next few months sales of "Maple Leaf Rag" were strong enough to encourage Stark and Joplin to move to St. Louis. The composition would go on to sell hundreds of thousands of copies over the next ten years, establishing Joplin as "The King of the Ragtime Writers." "Maple Leaf Rag" lives on as the definitive ragtime composition—the benchmark by which all other classic rags are judged.

John Stark was Joplin's primary publisher and a life-long champion of classic ragtime. He used the money he made from Joplin's "Maple Leaf Rag" to buy a printing press and establish his publishing company.

James Scott (1886–1938)

Nicknamed "the little professor," James Scott is generally recognized as classic ragtime's second greatest composer, next to Scott Joplin. Like Joplin, Scott was a tireless composer who believed that ragtime should transcend the sporting houses in which it was born and make its way into the salons and concert halls of polite society.

James Scott began his musical training as a young boy in Neosho, Missouri. Born with perfect pitch, Scott quickly picked up songs on his family's old, battered reed organ. One of the Scotts' neighbors, an elderly black man named John Coleman, recognized talent in the young boy and taught James to play the piano and to read music.

The Scotts eventually moved to Carthage, where, at the age of sixteen, James got a job as a window washer in the Dumars Music Store. One day the owner discovered James playing one of the pianos in the storeroom. Since he could play extremely well and could read music, Dumars hired the boy to plug sheet music in the store.

One year later, Dumars entered the publishing business with James Scott's first composition, "A Summer Breeze—March and Two Step." Scott was only seventeen years old. He quickly followed that piece with "Fascinator March" and "On the Pike— March and Two Step," a song written in celebration of the St. Louis Exposition.

The year of the exposition, Scott took a pilgrimage to St. Louis to meet Scott Joplin. Joplin was so impressed by the younger man's compositions and playing that he took him into his inner circle of ragtimers, along with Scott Hayden and Arthur Marshall. Joplin also introduced James Scott to John Stark, who became Scott's primary publisher for the rest of his career.

In 1906, Stark published one of Scott's finest compositions, "Frog Legs." Stark wrote: "Now we need adjectives in fifteen degrees with a rising inflection. We need letters a foot high and a few exclamation points about the size of Cleopatra's needle—but we won't tell you of this piece, we want to surprise you."

Scott was an extremely prolific composer, who published more than thirty rags between 1903 and 1922, and most likely wrote dozens more. Each piece grew increasingly more complicated, and it is unlikely that any publisher other than John Stark would have published sheet music for rags that were so difficult to play. Scott also recorded fourteen piano rolls of his compositions, many of which sounded like two people playing at once.

Although Scott never became a rich man from his compositions—he lived comfortably off of money he made teaching piano and playing in a Kansas City movie theater—he is credited with writing some of the finest rags of all time, including "Great Scott Rag" (1909), "Climax Rag" (1914), "Evergreen Rag" (1915), " Prosperity Rag" (1916), and "Honeymoon Rag" (1916).

His cousin Patsy Thomas said, "Jimmy never talked about his music, just wrote, wrote, wrote, and played it for anyone who would listen. He wrote music as fluently as writing a letter, humming and writing all at the same time."

Tom Turpin
and the Rosebud Cafe

St. Louis, with its strategic perch on the banks of the Mississippi River, was a prosperous industrial city and the unofficial capital of the Midwest. Like any large city at the time, St. Louis had a well-established and thriving sporting district, where traveling businessmen, cattlemen, and locals would come to drink, gamble, and pick up prostitutes. St. Louis' large red-light district was also a lucrative haven for musicians. Every block had three saloons, every saloon housed a piano, and every piano had to play continuously from sundown to sunup.

By 1901, the ragtime craze had already begun to sweep the nation. That year Joplin wrote "Sunflower Slow Drag," "Peacherine Rag," "The Easy Winners," and "Augustine Club Waltzes," all of which were published by John Stark. Joplin also completed a non-ragtime vocal song with words by Henry Jackson called "I'm Thinking of My Pickinniny Days," which was published by Thiebes-Stierlin in St. Louis.

Many white ragtime pioneers also made their mark in the first few years of the twentieth century. Charles Hunter, a blind Nashville native who emigrated to St. Louis, had published "Tickled to Death—Ragtime March and Two Step," "A Tennessee Tantalizer," "'Possum and 'Taters—a Ragtime Feast," "Cotton Bolls," and "Queen of Love—Two Step." Thomas Broady, another Nashville writer, composed "Mandy's Broadway Stroll," "A Tennessee Jubilee," and "Whittling Remus Rag." The classically trained Charles L. Johnson published "Scandalous Thompson—Cake Walk," "Doc Brown's Cake Walk," and "Black Smoke—Dance Characteristic." In 1906, Johnson wrote the seminal ragtime hit "Dill Pickles Rag."

These were not the novelty rags and pale imitations that would soon be pouring from the pianos of the white Tin Pan Alley hacks. They were authentic ragtime syncopations very much in the African-American tradition.

The spiritual and artistic capital of ragtime was in the red-light district of St. Louis. And the epicenter of this was the Rosebud Cafe, owned and operated by a large, generous black man by the name of Thomas Million Turpin.

During the late 1890s and early 1900s, the St. Louis sporting district was the unofficial capital of ragtime and the home of such musical pioneers as Tom Turpin, Scott Joplin, Louis Chauvin, and James Scott.

Tom Turpin was born in 1873 in Savannah, Georgia, the second son of John and Lulu Turpin. "Honest John" Turpin was politically active during Reconstruction (a street in Savannah was named after the Turpin family), and he was proud of the fact that he never worked for another man after Emancipation. In the early 1880s the Turpin family—John, Lulu, eldest son Charles, Tom, and two young daughters—moved to St. Louis, where Honest John opened the Silver Dollar Saloon. John ran the Silver Dollar until 1903, when it was torn down to build a railroad station in anticipation of the St. Louis Exposition of 1904.

As a teenager, Tom taught himself to play the piano, and became quite accomplished despite his lack of formal training. The young Turpin, however, did not have the same musical drive as Scott Joplin or Otis Saunders. He saw music as a way of having fun and making money.

In 1885, Tom and Charles bought an interest in a gold mine and moved to Nevada for a few years. The mine yielded little gold, however, and the two were soon forced to return to St. Louis, where Tom opened the Rosebud.

Tom Turpin had already made his mark as the author of "Harlem Rag" (1897), the first published instrumental rag by an African-American composer. While Turpin published only four other rags in his lifetime—"The Bowery Buck" (1899), "A Ragtime Nightmare" (1900), "St. Louis Rag" (1903), and "The Buffalo Rag" (1904)—his influence on the development of ragtime was immeasurable. The Rosebud Cafe was a regular haunt of St. Louis' best rag players, and was the first stop of any musician traveling through the River City.

Many of ragtime's greatest performers and innovators went on to become famous jazz musicians. The Cotton Club, in Harlem, was the premiere showcase for the exciting new musical form.

The Rosebud consisted of a bar in front, a "hotel" upstairs, and a wine room in the back, which was accessible from the bar or from a side "family entrance." It was in the wine room that Turpin held court around a battered upright piano. The more serious "cutting" sessions, however, were held across the street at Mother Johnson's house. Whenever a new hotshot piano player came to town, Turpin would take him across the street to test his licks.

By the turn of the century, the Rosebud was the unofficial clubhouse of many of ragtime's greatest performers, including Joe Jordan ("Double Fudge—Ragtime Two Step," "Nappy Lee," "The Darkey Todalo"), Charlie Warfield ("I Ain't Got Nobody," "Baby, Won't You Please Come Home"), Sam Patterson ("Dandy Coon," "The Moon Is Shining in the Skies"), and the legendary Louis Chauvin.

Louis Chauvin was only seventeen when he and his next-door neighbor, Sam Patterson, first wandered into the Rosebud Cafe. Impressed by the duo's musical abilities, Turpin set about teaching Chauvin and Patterson the basics of ragtime. It wasn't too long before Chauvin was playing circles around his mentor.

For the landmark book *They All Played Ragtime*, author Rudi Blesh interviewed Patterson about Chauvin's immense talent: "As a boy I thought I was some peanuts, but I knew then I would not be the artist Chauv was....I only played the style of rags that Tom Turpin wrote. Chauvin didn't play that style—he would change them....Turpin was great, but Chauvin could do things Turpin couldn't touch."

Unfortunately for ragtime, Louis Chauvin liked the sporting life too much. Aside from a brief stint with Sam Patterson as a two-man music/comedy team, Chauvin spent much of his time in the red-light districts of St. Louis and Chicago, descending into a life of hard drinking and womanizing. Chauvin never published a rag on his own; his only

The legendary Louis Chauvin was considered one of the greatest ragtime players by his peers. Unfortunately, he never published any of his compositions.

published ragtime composition was the hauntingly beautiful introduction to Scott Joplin's "Heliotrope Bouquet" (1907). According to Patterson, Chauvin was an accomplished composer, but he never bothered to write any of his compositions down: "He would sit right down and compose a number with three or four strains. By tomorrow it was gone and he'd compose another....Chauv was so far ahead with his modern stuff, he would be up to date now."

Ragtime originally developed in the sporting houses of the midwest. Here, a "cocotte" entertains three men in the Chicago red-light district.

Louis Chauvin died in Chicago on March 26, 1908, at the age of twenty-five after slipping into a coma from an opium overdose; he never fulfilled the promise of his musical genius. His lack of published material and the fact that he never made any piano rolls means that there is no record of the person who many believed was the greatest ragtime player of all.

Joplin was not to fall victim to same excesses as Chauvin. After moving to St. Louis, the newly married Joplin gave up the sporting life for good. While he kept in touch with Turpin and the rest of the St. Louis ragtime scene, Joplin never again made his living by playing the honky-tonks and saloons. Instead he set himself up as a teacher and lived off the royalties from "Maple Leaf Rag" and his other compositions.

John Stark, in turn, used the money he made from "Maple Leaf Rag" to buy a printing press in St. Louis. He now had the freedom to set up a full-fledged music publishing business—specializing in classic ragtime music.

St. Louis was the base of operations for Joplin until 1907. His years there were the most productive years of his life. The fame and financial security that Joplin enjoyed from the success of "Maple Leaf Rag" allowed him to devote all his time to composing new music. While he was in St. Louis, Joplin published more than twenty rags (including "Elite Syncopations," "The Cascades," and "The Entertainer"), six vocal songs, and a ragtime ballet ("The Ragtime Dance"). Joplin also began work on what would become his life's obsession: *Treemonisha*, a full-length opera written in ragtime. Joplin had written a shorter ragtime opera in

1903 called *A Guest of Honor.* While this opera went unpublished, portions of it were performed in St. Louis. The manuscript for this work, however, has been lost since Joplin's death, and it is unclear whether parts of it were the bases of some of his later ragtime pieces.

Projects such as a ragtime ballet and a ragtime opera are indicative of just how serious Joplin was about his music. He was a

Scott Joplin spent his entire life trying gain respect for his music. "Bethena" was the first of two syncopated concert waltzes that he wrote.

dedicated composer whose ambitions rose above the popular music form that ragtime had become. Joplin's unflappable dedication to his music, however, conflicted greatly with the image of ragtime.

For the rest of America, ragtime music was good-time music. With the advent of the Pianola and then the player piano, it was fast becoming big business as well. In New York City, the Tin Pan Alley song factories were well aware of the commercial possibilities of ragtime. As Scott Joplin sat behind his piano in St. Louis, working feverishly on his opera, hundreds of Tin Pan Alley hacks were busy simplifying and homogenizing ragtime, making it easier to play, catchier to hum, and more palatable to mainstream America.

The player piano made it easy for anyone to "play" the complicated syncopations of ragtime. Ragtime composers often recorded the piano rolls of their material.

Tin Pan Alley, Irving Berlin, and the Selling of Ragtime

The first fifteen years of the twentieth century were truly the era of sheet music. A piano in the parlor was the status symbol of a well-bred, cultured family. In addition, vaudeville was taking off as the premier form of family entertainment. Singers such as Al Jolson (1886–1950), Sophie Tucker (1884–1966), Harrigan and Hart, Norah Baynes, and Lillian Russell (1861–1922) were the stars of the era, and everyone with a piano wanted to play these stars' latest hits. Beyond piano rolls for the player piano, there was no recorded music at the time, so sheet music was the only way of getting the hits of the day into the American home.

Prior to the 1890s, the music publishing industry was spread out across the country, with established publishers based in St. Louis, Cincinnati, Chicago, Baltimore, Philadelphia, and Boston. Songwriters sought out publishers to buy and publish their latest tune. Often publishers would charge singers for the honor of having their likenesses printed on the first page of the latest hit songs; the singers could then use the sheet music as calling cards.

As the popularity of vaudeville grew—and its performers became big stars—so did the sheet music industry. Between vaudeville and the theater, New York was the entertainment capital of America. By the 1890s, it was the music publishing capital as well.

The publishing industry as it developed in New York was not the genteel business of years past. These were not small publishers who carefully sifted through the latest creations of independent songwriters, looking for quality as well as commercial viability. The New York publishers were literally song factories. Large companies such as Witmark & Sons, E.B. Marks, Jerome H. Remick & Co., Harry Von Tilzer Publishing Company, and the Ted Snyder Music Company lined Twenty-eighth Street, each with scores of songwriters under contract. These tunesmiths populated a beehive of small rooms with pianos and would spend day and night pounding out what they hoped would be the latest hits of the day. Twenty-eighth Street was dubbed Tin Pan Alley for the tinny clang of the pianos coming from the open windows.

One of the strategies of the Tin Pan Alley publishers was to give popular performers songwriting credits (as well as royalties) for songs so that they would sing them in their shows. Al Jolson was one of the biggest benefactors of this practice. He received songwriting credit and

Tin Pan Alley publishers often gave popular singers writing credit and royalties for songs in exchange for the right to use their likenesses on the cover of the sheet music.

royalties for songs such as "Me and My Shadow" and "The Anniversary Song," though he never wrote a note of music or a lyric in his life. This was one of the earliest forms of music industry payola.

In 1884, Willis Woodward offered songwriting credit for "Always Take My Mother's Advice" to a teenage minstrel singer named Julius Witmark. While Witmark never collected many royalties on the tune, he and his brothers earned enough from the vaudeville circuit to buy Woodward's company two years later, forming Witmark & Sons. The

Eubie Blake (1883–1983)

James Herbert "Eubie" Blake enjoyed one of the longest careers in the history of American popular music—a career that began in 1899, when the sixteen-year-old Eubie began playing the cafes of his native Baltimore, and ended with his death eighty-four years later, five days after Eubie's one hundredth birthday.

Eubie was taught to play music by W. Llewellyn Wilson, one of the most influential music teachers of all time. At one point during the 1920s, all of the black music teachers in New York City, as well as many black performers, were former Wilson students.

Despite Eubie's natural talent, his mother never approved of Eubie's music. She was an extremely religious woman who did not approve of any type of secular music. Eubie, however, loved ragtime, and as a teenager he would sneak out of the house at night to go play piano in the tenderloin.

Eubie's early influences were the Baltimore march kings Big-Head Wilbur and Jimmy Green, as well as the man Eubie believed was the greatest ragtime player of all, One-Leg Willie Joseph.

Eubie honed his talents in the Baltimore red light district, but he was more drawn to the musical theater, so he moved to New York to try and publish a few of his early rag compositions and to try and work his way into vaudeville.

He took "Charleston Rag" and "Black Keys on Parade" to the Tin Pan Alley Publisher Joseph Stern, who was impressed with the pieces, but was hesitant to publish anything by a black composer. The belief was that no one would buy music by a black songwriter. Stern also felt that Eubie's music was much too complicated. In 1914, Stern finally agreed to publish two of Eubie's rags, "Chevy

Chase" and "Fizz Water," but only if Eubie agreed to simplify the scores and eliminate some of the syncopation. This was a trend that would haunt Blake's career. Many of his finest ragtime piano solos were never published because they were too difficult to play.

In 1915, Eubie Blake teamed up with the gifted lyricist, singer, and entertainer Noble Sissle, beginning one of the most successful collaborations in American music. The two toured Europe as part of James Reese

In 1915, Eubie Blake teamed up with the talented singer and lyricist Noble Sissle. The two hit it big in 1921 with their musical review <u>Shuffle Along</u>.

Europe's band and then returned to New York to write and produce the smash hit musical review *Shuffle Along* in 1921. *Shuffle Along* generated many hit songs for Blake and Sissle, including "I'm Just Wild About Harry," "Love Will Find A Way," "Bandanna Days," and "Gypsy Blues." A year later the two collaborated on another hit show, *Chocolate Dandies*, but their collaboration ended in 1927 when Sissle wanted to continue a tour of Europe and Blake wanted to return home.

Although he only published six ragtime pieces during the heyday of ragtime, Blake was universally recognized as one of the music's finest players, as well as one of its greatest storytellers. Blake's view of ragtime, however, was far less restrictive than that of Scott Joplin, John Stark, or James Scott. He once said, "Anything that is syncopated is basically ragtime. I don't care whether it's Liszt's *Hungarian Rhapsody* or Tchaikovsky in his *Waltz of the Flowers*."

brothers used their father's name in the company (they were the "Sons") because they were all underage. In the heyday of New York music publishers, Witmark & Sons was the most powerful on Tin Pan Alley.

Another strategy of the Alleymen was to lower the price of sheet music, hoping that the volume would make up for the loss of margin. In the late 1800s, the average piece of sheet music cost around fifty cents. The Alleymen lowered that to ten cents and eventually a nickel. They also flooded the market with material. They were more willing to take chances on new styles of music and on marginal songs. The old guard of publishing companies from Boston and Chicago were extremely cautious about what songs they released. On Tin Pan Alley, however, publishers relied on volume. Their thinking was that if you released enough product, at least one song was sure to become a hit.

Tin Pan Alley wasn't interested in publishing high art; companies like Witmark & Sons knew there was big money in publishing the songs of the common people. The real gift of these streetwise tunesmiths was in their ability to assess the latest trends and styles of music, figure out what would become popular in the next year or two, then imitate and simplify that music, making it accessible to the general public.

The Alleymen saw the potential for huge sales in ragtime music. "Maple Leaf Rag" had sold hundreds of thousands of copies with little more than word-of-mouth advertising—and this was an instrumental tune written by a black man. Ragtime was an infectious, happy form of music, full of energy and excitement. The only problems with it—according to the Alleymen—were that it was instrumental and it was just too difficult to play.

Tin Pan Alley hit new heights riding on the back of ragtime. The revamped sound was a commercialized, watered-down style played by white musicians who learned it from blacks. Just as white performers popularized black folk music with minstrelsy, Tin Pan Alley took over ragtime music and created a music craze the likes of which the country had never before seen. (This is a phenomenon that would repeat itself throughout the history of American popular music, with such forms as jazz, swing, the blues, and rock and roll: black musicians would pioneer a new style of music only to have whites sanitize it, make it popular, and rake in the profits.)

The first step in making ragtime more popular was to simplify the heavy piano syncopation played with the right hand. Next the Alleymen added lyrics, creating the ragtime song. The first few Tin Pan Alley ragtime hits were either standard instrumental ragtime hits with words added or novelty ragtime versions of well-known tunes.

Al Jolson, right, on the golf course with Irving Berlin—two Russian immigrants who made it big in the heyday of Tin Pan Alley.

With the hit song "Alexander's Ragtime Band" Irving Berlin became known as the "King of Ragtime," although he later admitted that he never really knew what ragtime was.

In 1908, Ted Snyder (1881–1965) added words to an instrumental rag he had written years earlier called "Wild Cherries Rag." While the original version of the song had been a flop, the new vocal version of the tune sold more than one million copies.

The man who was most responsible for creating the national ragtime craze was a young Russian immigrant named Israel Baline (1888–1989), otherwise known as Irving Berlin. Born on May 11, 1888, in Tyumen, an illegal Jewish settlement in the middle of Siberia, Israel Baline was one of eight children of Leah and Moses Baline. When Israel was just four years old, the Baline family—minus two sons who decided to stay—fled to New York to escape the state-sanctioned religious persecution of Jews. As a teenager, Israel became enamored with the nightclubs and vaudeville theaters of the Bowery. A poor student who was always getting into trouble, Israel quit school as a teenager to wait tables and sing for nickels at Bowery beer halls and saloons such as Callahan's, the Choo-Choo Palace, and MacLears. Before long, Israel was such an established presence on the bar circuit that Tin Pan Alley publisher Harry Von Tilzer hired him to plug songs on the Bowery.

It was while working for Von Tilzer that Baline met pianist Ted Snyder, beginning a long and fruitful partnership. Baline's first song was "Marie from Sunny Italy." Due to a printer's error, however, he was listed as "I. Berlin" on the sheet music. Israel decided then to shed his Jewish name for the flashier Irving Berlin.

Two of Berlin's greatest talents were that he was a wonderful mimic and a hilarious parodist. He was able to take popular songs and current situations and put a funny twist to them. Initially, Berlin was solely a lyricist, with Snyder writing the music or the two of them "borrowing" the music from elsewhere, but he eventually learned to play the piano and write his own music.

Between 1908 and 1911, Berlin scored several ragtime song hits: "That Mesmerizing Mendelsson Tune" (a ragtime version of "Spring Song"), "Yiddle Your Fiddle, Let's Play Some Ragtime" (combining what Alleymen called a "yid" song with ragtime), "That Mysterious Rag," "Ragtime Violin," and "The Grizzly Bear" (a George Botsford instrumental rag set to words). Berlin's and Tin Pan Alley's biggest hit came in 1911, when the songwriter dusted off and added words to an old march he had written and abandoned a few years back called "Alexander's Ragtime Band."

Originally written as an instrumental, "Alexander's Ragtime Band" was an attempt by Berlin to write a song that was a little more serious than the comic tunes he and Snyder were churning out at the time. The song's first public performance was at a cabaret in the theater district. It was so poorly received that they never bothered publishing it. In 1911, Berlin reworked the song for *The Frolic of the Friars*, the yearly benefit performance at the Friar's Club, a show-business fraternity. Again it received a lukewarm reception, but this time Snyder decided to publish it.

The song was next used in *The Merry Whirl*, a Broadway musical comedy revue. *The Merry Whirl* turned out to be the surprise hit of the summer, and "Alexander's Ragtime Band" was the show's big hit. Vaudeville stars such as Emma Carus and Al Jolson picked up the song, and soon it was sweeping the nation.

By 1912, "Alexander's Ragtime Band" had sold more than two million copies and Irving Berlin was being hailed as the "King of Ragtime." Because of the immense success of this song, the world came to believe that Berlin was the inventor of the music, that he had written every ragtime hit. Ironically, Berlin later admitted that he never really understood what ragtime was. Certainly, "Alexander's Ragtime Band" had little to do with the music of Scott Joplin and Tom Turpin. Rhythmically it is a straight march with no syncopation in it whatsoever. But America didn't seem to care—it was caught up in the spirit of ragtime, if not the reality of it.

Treemonisha

At the same time that Irving Berlin was being wrongly hailed as the "King of Ragtime," the true practitioners of syncopated music were hitting hard times. In the years leading up to World War I, classic ragtime

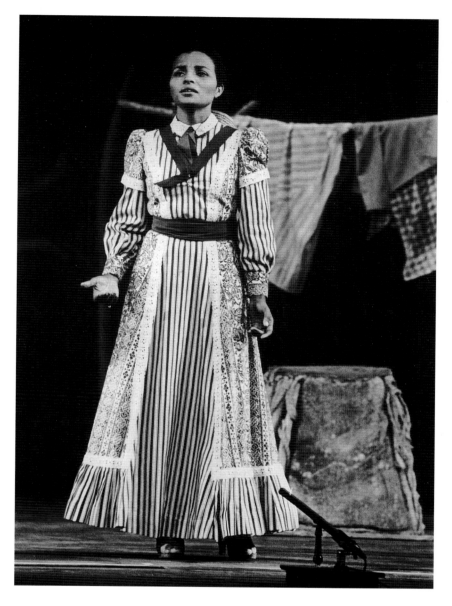

Carmen Balthrop performs in the Houston Grand Opera company production of <u>Treemonisha</u>, fifty years after Scott Joplin's death.

was eclipsed by the novelty rags of Tin Pan Alley. The early ragtime players were either dying or giving up, and younger generations of African-American musicians were turning to a new form of popular music known as jazz.

Scott Joplin moved to New York in 1907, as John Stark had two years earlier. While Joplin continued to write many quality rags during his first years in New York ("Gladiolus Rag," "Pineapple Rag," "Euphonic Sounds," and "Scott Joplin's New Rag," to name a few) his obsession became the writing and publication of *Treemonisha*, his ragtime opera. It was also during this time that Joplin had a falling out with Stark, partially due to the fact that Stark refused to publish anything as commercially unviable as a ragtime opera, but mostly due to Joplin's increasing moodiness and paranoia. The composer was prone to fits of depression, which were sometimes so severe that he was unable to play his piano.

After 1910, Joplin worked on little else besides his opera. Stark and other publishers would occasionally come out with a new Joplin rag, but more often than not it was a release of something Joplin had written years before or one of the pieces from *Treemonisha*.

Treemonisha contains twenty-seven complete musical numbers and a libretto of more than two hundred pages. When he finally completed this massive work, Joplin tried in vain to find a publisher who would be willing to release it. When he finally concluded that no one wanted to handle it, he went ahead and published it at his own expense in 1911 under the Scott Joplin Music Company imprint. Once he had it published, Joplin spent the rest of his life and all his money in a fruitless and demoralizing attempt to get *Treemonisha* produced onstage. Over the next six years his mental condition grew progressivedly worse. On April 11, 1917, the last of his sanity gone, Scott Joplin died in a hospital bed in Astoria, New York, at the age of forty-nine.

Despite his refusal to publish Joplin's ragtime opera, Stark remained one of the most ardent defenders of ragtime. However, things had not gone well for Stark since he moved to New York. His publishing style and his unshakable love of classic ragtime could not compete with the fast-paced hit factories of Tin Pan Alley. After his wife died in 1911, Stark moved his publishing base back to St. Louis—to the same printing press that had been paid for by "Maple Leaf Rag."

James P. Johnson (1894–1955)

James P. Johnson was one of New York's premier piano players, an important link between ragtime and jazz, and the inventor and chief practitioner of the New York stride style of piano. He inspired the great Duke Ellington and taught Fats Waller how to play.

Born in 1894 in New Brunswick, New Jersey, James P. Johnson moved to Jersey City with his family at an early age. While in Jersey City, the young boy was surrounded by all types of music. His mother sang in the church choir, and he heard the syncopated music from the saloons, the marching bands at parades and politician's rallies, and, at the age of eleven, he went across the river to New York with his brother to hear and see the New York Symphony. In *They All Played Ragtime* Rudi Blesh quotes Johnson as saying, "All I heard was music—from the old ditties the pimps passed on from ear to ear up to the long-hair stuff."

Johnson began taking piano lessons and learned how to play Joplin's "Gladiolus Rag." Johnson's family soon moved into New York City, where his mother bought him his first piano. Three years later he started his career playing rent parties. (In order to raise money to pay their rent, people would hold parties where they would charge an entrance fee in exchange for food, drink, dancing, and musical entertainment.)

It was at these rent parties that Johnson came in contact with black seamen and longshoreman from the southern coast ports. Johnson was particularly influenced by the Gullahs of the Sea Islands of Carolina and Georgia who spoke a dialect that included aspects of both African languages and English. In 1928, Johnson wrote a symphonic piece called *Yamekraw*, which was inspired by the Gullahs.

Throughout the 1910s and 1920s Johnson was known as the king of stride piano, a form of ragtime that featured a complicated walking bass line as well as a syncopated melody. His piece "Carolina Shout" (1925) was the yardstick by which all New York rag and stride players were measured. Fats Waller learned the piece by buying the piano roll recorded by Johnson and then slowing it down so that he could pick out each note and inflection.

In 1923, Waller and Johnson collaborated on a musical review called *Shuffling Along*. Hits from that show included "Snowy Morning," "Keep off the Grass," and "Charleston," which inspired the greatest dance craze of the 1920s.

During the 1930s, Johnson concentrated almost exclusively on writing serious music. He was able to live comfortably off of his royalties, and he dedicated himself to symphonic pieces such as *Symphony Harlem*, *Yamekraw: A Negro Rhapsody*, and *De Organiser*, a short opera he wrote with poet Langston Hughes.

Unfortunately much of Johnson's later work was lost due to lack of interest from the white publishing community. It is for his stride and ragtime playing that Johnson is best known. His technical skill at the keyboard was only equaled by the likes of jazz musicians Art Tatum and Earl Hines.

By the 1920s, ragtime had given way to jazz as the country's premier form of popular music. The first and perhaps most influential solo star in jazz was Louis Armstrong.

Back in St. Louis, Stark went back to the style of publishing he knew best; however, Joplin was no longer his lead writer. Stark now relied on artists such as Joe Lamb ("Ethiopia Rag," "Cleopatra Rag," "The Ragtime Nightingale," "Bohemia Rag"), James Scott ("Hilarity Rag," "Kansas City Rag," "New Era Rag"), and Artie Mathews ("Pastime Rag," numbers 1 through 4) for the majority of his income. While sales for these classic rags remained steady, ragtime music was clearly not the phenomenon it had been ten years earlier.

John Stark continued his publishing efforts into the 1920s, but by 1922—the year Tom Turpin died—ragtime was nothing more than a quaint nostalgic genre. Jazz was the newest thing, and exciting musicians such as Jelly Roll Morton (1885–1941), Fats Waller (1904–1943), and Eubie Blake—all of whom had helped to popularize ragtime—were busy breaking new musical ground just as Scott Joplin and Tom Turpin had done before them.

Even then, however, ragtime was not completely gone. Strains of the syncopation and rhythm that gave ragtime its character were very much in evidence in the jazz and swing of the 1920s and 1930s. In the 1950s ragtime enjoyed a brief resurgence as musicians such as

In the 1960s pianist Max Morath led a ragtime revival with a television special, <u>The Ragtime Era</u> (1960), and two touring shows, "Ragtime Revisited" and "Max Morath at the Turn of the Century."

Knuckles O'Toole, Lou Busch, Johnny Maddox, Winifred Atwell, Max Morath, and Bill Bolcom revived the music of Joplin and finally gave him credit for being the true king of ragtime.

In 1973, ragtime had another revival when Gunther Schuller played several of Joplin's compositions for the soundtrack of the film *The Sting*. Joplin once said that maybe his music would be appreciated fifty years after his death. Fifty-six years after his death he scored a top-ten hit with "The Entertainer," and in 1976 the Houston Grand Opera staged *Treemonisha*, thus fulfilling Joplin's lifelong ambition.

Conclusion

Born in the 1890s in the sporting districts of midwestern cities, and with musical roots that went back to the days of slavery and beyond, ragtime music was one of the first original American forms of popular music and *the* first popular music that came directly from African American music. Ragtime was the forerunner of jazz and the blues, and for a time was the most popular and compelling form of music on the planet.

While the publishers and song writing hacks of Tin Pan Alley sanitized and simplified ragtime in order to churn out reams and reams of sheet music, it is the inspired music of the true ragtime artists such as Scott Joplin, James Scott, Joseph Lamb, John Stark, James P. Johnson, and Eubie Blake that stretched the musical boundaries of ragtime and transformed what was essentially good-time drinking music into a valid and influential musical art form.

John Stark put it best in an advertisement he distributed for his publishing company in 1916:

> *"As Pike's Peak to a mole hill, so are our rag classics to*
> *the slush that fills the jobber's bulletins. As the language*

Eubie Blake was a rag piano player, bandleader, composer, and storyteller whose career lasted more than eighty years, passing through every major musical movement of the twentieth century.

of the college graduate in thought and expression to the gibberage of the Alley Toot....This old world rolled around on its axis many long, long years before people learned that it was not flat. Then they wanted to kill the man that discovered it....The brightest minds of all civilized countries are now grading many of the [classic] rags with the finest musical creations of all time. They cannot be interpreted at sight. They must be studied and practiced slowly....[classic rags] are the musical advanced thought of this age, and America's only creation."

Listener's Guide

Blake, Eubie. *Memories of You.* Biograph Records.

Blake, Eubie. *Tricky Fingers.* Quicksilver Records.

Castle, Jo Anne. *22 Greatest Ragtime Hits.* Ranwood.

Castle, Jo Anne. *Ragtime Piano Gal.* Ranwood.

Elite Syncopators. *Ragtime Special.* Stomp Off.

Hazelton, Tom. *Ragtime's Greatest Hits.* Pro Arte.

Johnson, James P. *Carolina Shout.* Biograph Records.

Johnson, James P. *Snowy Morning Blues.* UNI/GRP.

Joplin, Scott. *Complete Works of Scott Joplin.* Laserlight.

Joplin, Scott. *King of The Ragtime Writers.* Biograph Records.

Joplin, Scott. *The Original Piano Rolls: 1896–1917.* Accord.

Morath, Max. *Ragtime Man.* Omega Classics.

Morath, Max & the Ragtime Quintet. *Ragtime Women.* Vangaurd.

Morton, Jelly Roll. *Complete Victor Recordings.* BMG/RCA.

Morton, Jelly Roll. *Mr. Jelly Lord.* Rhino Records.

Rose, Wally. *Ragtime Classics.* Good Time Jazz.

Whitcomb, Ian. *Ragtime America.* Audiophile.

Further Reading

Barrett, Mary Ellin. *Irving Berlin: A Daughter's Memoir.* Simon and Schuster, 1994.

Berlin, Edward A. *King of Ragtime: Scott Joplin and His Era.* Oxford University Press, 1994.

———. *Ragtime: A Musical and Cultural History.* University of California Press, 1984.

Berlin, Irving. *Songs of Irving Berlin: Ragtime and Early Songs.* Hal Leonord Publishing Corporation, 1991.

Blesh, Rudi, and Harriet Janis. *They All Played Ragtime.* Alfred A. Knopf, 1950.

Budger, Reid. *A Life in Ragtime: A Biography of James Reese Europe.* Oxford University Press, 1995.

Clarke, Donald, ed. *The Penguin Encyclopedia of Popular Music.* Viking/Penguin, 1989.

Clarke, Donald. *The Rise and Fall of Popular Music.* St. Martin's Press, 1995.

Jasen, David A., and Trebor Tichenor. *Rags & Ragtime: A Musical History.* Dover, 1989.

Morgan, Thomas L. *From Cakewalks to Concert Halls: An Illustrated History of African American Pop Music from 1895 to 1930.* Elliot & Clask Publications, 1993.

Waldo, T. *This Is Ragtime.* Da Capo/Plenum Trade, 1991.

Whitcomb, Ian. *Irving Berlin & Ragtime America.* Limelight Edition, 1988.

Witmark, Isidore, and Isaac Goldberg. *From Ragtime to Swingtime: The Story of the House of Witmark.* Lee Furman, 1939.

Photography Credits

©Archive Photos: 13, 15, 45, 57

©Archive Photos/Frank Driggs Collection: front cover (inset), 28

©Associated Press: 8, 51

©Bettmann Archive: 10, 12, 23, 24, 38, 42, 44

Bloch, Albert. *Ragtime.* ©Christie's, London/Superstock: 2

Cucuel, Edward. *Cakewalk by Black Americans.* ©A.K.G., Berlin/Superstock: 18

©Frank Driggs Collection: 17, 19, 21, 31, 32, 34, 35, 36, 41, 48-49, 59

©Everett Collection: 58

©Everett Collection/C.S.U. Archives: 27

©Globe Photos: 47, 61

©Jon Hammer/Archive Photos: 22

©Neil Nissing/FPG: 7

©North Wind Picture Archive: 9, 11, 14

©Photofest: 39, 52, 55

©UPI/Bettmann: front cover (background), 16

Index